Book/Accompaniment CDs

CW00538447

SCHIRMER'S LIBRARY
OF MUSICAL CLASSICS

Vol. 1747-B

Masterworks
for
Clarinet and Piano

By
Weber, Schumann,
Mendelssohn, and Brahms

Edited by Eric Simon

On the accompaniment recording:
STEFANIE JACOB and **ELENA ABEND**

ISBN 978-1-61780-634-6

G. SCHIRMER, Inc.

DISTRIBUTED BY

HAL•LEONARD®
CORPORATION
7777 W. BLUEMOUND RD. P.O. BOX 13819 MILWAUKEE, WI 53213

www.schirmer.com
www.halleonard.com

PREFACE

The clarinet was invented around the year 1700, and has since then been gradually developed and improved. The significant works for clarinet and piano written in the 19th century (the period covered in the present volume) are few in number, but rich in technical and expressive range.

While the works of Schumann and Brahms for clarinet and piano have been published and reprinted in satisfactory editions, the works of Weber have been over-edited since their first publication. The Mendelssohn Sonata was first published in 1941, in a slightly revised form.

Composers have been inspired in writing for the clarinet by great clarinet players. Mozart wrote for Stadler, Brahms for Mühlfeld, and Weber for Heinrich Bärmann. Weber's clarinet works were later revised by Bärmann's son Carl, the author of a clarinet method and studies. It is in Carl Bärmann's edition that they are best known. Jähns, in his Weber Catalogue, says: "This revision became . . . very important for these works, since it is based on the traditions which Carl Bärmann received from his father Heinrich regarding the execution and the contents of the compositions, which had been partly distorted."

The present editor has in his possession a Photostat of the first edition of Weber's Variations, with marginal notes by Jähns. On page 4, Jähns writes: "Variation III, according to a letter from Carl Bärmann to me, dated October 31, 1864, is composed by his father. As the son says, these variations were really composed by Weber in collaboration with the father, particularly the third variation, *Adagio*. He also states: 'As far as I recall my father's story, they composed it one night in Prague on the eve of a big party where it was played for the first time.' This is in accordance with an entry in Weber's diary, reading: '1811, Dec. 14, morning; composed Variations in B-flat on a theme from *Silvana* for clarinet and piano; played it at night at Firmian's.'"

Let us compare the first two measure of the Variations in the original and in the Bärmann version.

Original   Bärmann

It is apparent that the Bärmann version leads to exaggerated phrasing, while the original version is more in keeping with the simplicity of the theme. Similar differences of interpretation are found on every page of Weber's clarinet compositions as edited by Bärmann.

In this edition we present Weber's clarinet works in their original form.

All deviations from the original manuscripts and from the basic editions are clearly marked. The editor's additions are put in brackets, and suggested omissions in parentheses. Otherwise, changes are limited to notation only. Suggested breath marks have been added to the clarinet part.

Weber's Grand Duo Concertant for Clarinet and Piano was composed in 1815–16. It is his last work for clarinet. Our edition is based on the autograph, now in the Library of Congress, and on the first edition.

Weber's Seven Variations for Clarinet and Piano on a theme from his opera *Silvana* were composed in 1811. Our edition is based on a copy of the first edition in the Berlin State Library, with Jähns' notes marking deviations from Weber's autograph.

Schuman's Fantasy-Pieces for Clarinet and Piano were composed in 1849. The present edition is based on Clara Schumann's edition, published by Breitkopf & Härtel. Schumann's autograph, bearing the title Soiréestücke, is in the Library of the Paris Conservatory. The most important discrepancies between the original manuscript and our edition should be noted: in the first piece, measures 2–19 are repeated (with 1st and 2nd endings); between the third and fourth measures from the end, an extra measure is inserted. In the manuscript the last two chords of the second piece are omitted.

Mendelssohn's Clarinet Sonata was composed about 1825. The present edition is the first and the only unabridged one. It follows the composer's autograph, which at present is in a private collection in the United States.

Brahms' Two Sonatas for Clarinet and Piano were composed in 1894, and published in 1895. Our edition follows the first edition, which was supervised by the composer himself.

E. S.

CONTENTS

Pianists on the CDs:
[1] Stefanie Jacob
[2] Elena Abend

Grand Duo Concertant
for Clarinet and Piano, Op. 48

Carl Maria von Weber
(1786–1826)

6

Andante con moto

RONDO
Allegro

Variations
for Clarinet and Piano, Op. 33

Carl Maria von Weber
(1786–1826)

Theme

Variation I

[L'istesso tempo]

Variation II

Con grazia

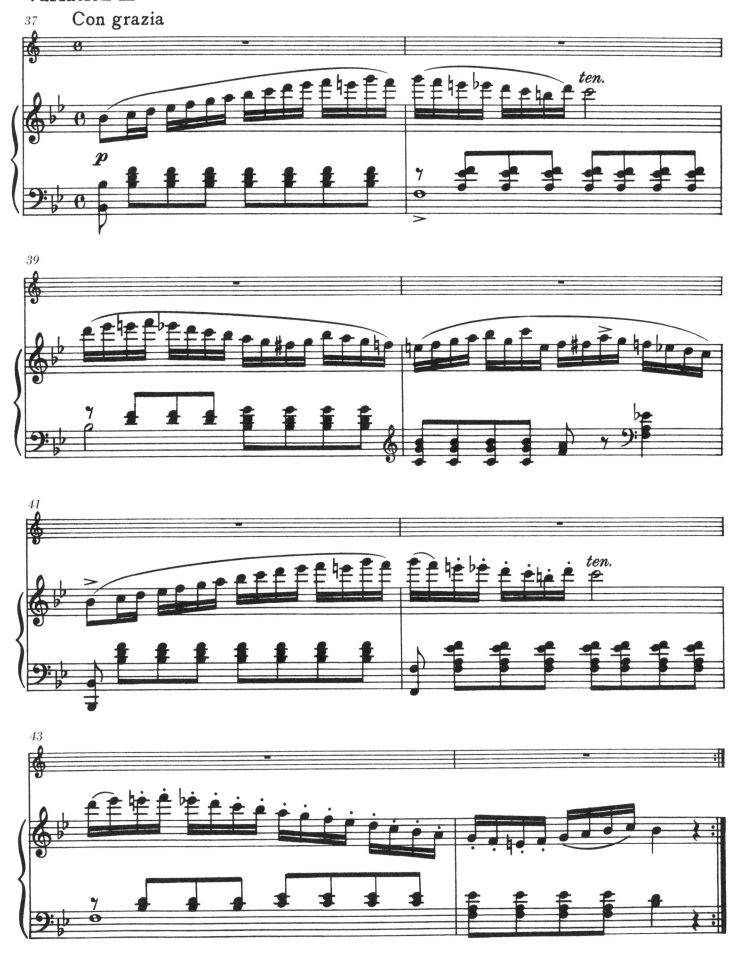

Variation III
Poco adagio

34

Variation IV
Tempo primo
animato e con fuoco

Variation V

[L'istesso tempo]

38

Variation VI

Variation VII

Dedicated to Andreas Grabau

Fantasy-Pieces
for Clarinet and Piano, Op. 73

1.

Robert Schumann
(1810–1856)

44

2.

Lebhaft, leicht ($\quad$ = 138)
(Vivace, leggero)

Coda
Nach und nach ruhiger
(Poco a poco più tranquillo)

3.

Rasch und mit Feuer (♩ = 160)
(Allegro con brio)

Sonata in E-flat Major

for Clarinet and Piano

Felix Mendelssohn
(1809–1847)

★ Vi - de indicates cuts suggested by the editor.

Original reads:

* Original reads:

78

Allegro moderato

★ This repeat is omitted on the recording.

Sonata No. 1 in F minor
for Clarinet and Piano, Op. 120, No. 1

Johannes Brahms
(1833–1897)

Allegretto grazioso

Sonata No. 2 in E-flat Major
for Clarinet and Piano, Op. 120, No. 2

Johannes Brahms
(1833–1897)

148

ABOUT THE ENHANCED CDs

In addition to piano accompaniments playable on both your CD player and computer, these enhanced CDs also include tempo adjustment software for computer use only. This software, known as Amazing Slow Downer, was originally created for use in pop music to allow singers and players the freedom to independently adjust both tempo and pitch elements. Because we believe there may be valuable uses for these features in other musical genres, we have included this software as a tool for both the teacher and student. For quick and easy installation instructions of this software, please see below.

In recording a piano accompaniment we necessarily must choose one tempo. Our choice of tempo, phrasing, and dynamics is carefully considered. But by the nature of recording, it is only one option.

However, we encourage you to explore your own interpretive ideas, which may differ from our recordings. This software feature allows you to adjust the tempo up and down without affecting the pitch. We recommend that this tempo adjustment feature be used with care and insight.

The audio quality may be somewhat compromised when played through the Amazing Slow Downer. This compromise in quality will not be a factor in playing the CD audio track on a normal CD player or through another audio computer program.

INSTALLATION FROM DOWNLOAD:

For Windows (XP, Vista or 7):
1. Download and save the .zip file to your hard drive.
2. Extract the .zip file.
3. Open the "ASD Lite" folder.
4. Double-click "setup.exe" to run the installer and follow the on-screen instructions.

For Macintosh (OSX 10.4 and up):
1. Download and save the .dmg file to your hard drive.
2. Double-click the .dmg file to mount the "ASD Lite" volume.
3. Double-click the "ASD Lite" volume to see its contents.
4. Drag the "ASD Lite" application into the Application folder.

INSTALLATION FROM CD:

For Windows (XP, Vista or 7):
1. Load the CD-ROM into your CD-ROM drive.
2. Open your CD-ROM drive. You should see a folder named "Amazing Slow Downer." If you only see a list of tracks, you are looking at the audio portion of the disk and most likely do not have a multi-session capable CD-ROM.
3. Open the "Amazing Slow Downer" folder.
4. Double-click "setup.exe" to install the software from the CD-ROM to your hard disk. Follow the on-screen instructions to complete installation.
5. Go to "Start," "Programs" and find the "Amazing Slow Downer Lite" application. Note: To guarantee access to the CD-ROM drive, the user should be logged in as the "Administrator."

For Macintosh (OSX 10.4 or higher):
1. Load the CD-ROM into your CD-ROM drive.
2. Double-click on the data portion of the CD-ROM (which will have the Hal Leonard icon in red and be named as the book).
3. Open the "Amazing OS X" folder.
4. Double-click the "ASD Lite" application icon to run the software from the CD-ROM, or copy this file to your hard drive and run it from there.

MINIMUM SOFTWARE REQUIREMENTS:

For Windows (XP, Vista or 7):
Pentium Processor; Windows XP, Vista, or 7; 8 MB Application RAM; 8x Multi-Session CD-ROM drive

For Macintosh (OS X 10.4 or higher):
Power Macintosh or Intel Processor; Mac OS X 10.4 or higher; MB Application RAM; 8x Multi-Session CD-ROM drive